# Fab Phonics Games

The Learning Lady

Hello!

My name is Emma Spiers, The Learning Lady : )

I'm an Early Reading and Phonics Expert, with over 20 years' experience.

Like you, I'm dedicated to improving learning experiences for our youngest readers, using the most effective, but super simple, teaching methods.

No Printing, no laminating, just learning!

I've helped thousands of headteachers, teachers, teaching assistants and parents to:
> Instantly improve Reading and Phonics progress and outcomes
> Save Time & Money
> Develop in-house Expertise

**These Fab Phonics Games** have been written with you and your school in mind. They are all super simple, cost effective, and will neatly fit into your daily Letters and Sounds routine. The aim is to help you put a bit of sparkle back into your phonics lessons, without lots of resourcing and complicated explanations to make it happen!

**I've used these Fab Phonics Games** in many, many schools across the UK, with AMAZING results. I know that you and your children are going to **love** playing these games as much as I already have.

*The Learning Lady*

# Table of Contents

Oral Blending & Segmenting Game- What's The Word Mr Wolf? ...................................4

Oral Blending & Segmenting Game – I Hear With My Little Ear .................................5

Oral Blending & Segmenting- Missing Objects 'Magic' Game.................................6

Supermarket Phoneme Spotting Game.................................................7

Blending Practise- Rob the Robot .....................................................8

Blending Practise- Speedy Read Game .................................................9

Blending Practise- The Alien Pop Up Game ..........................................10

Blending Practise- Tracking..........................................................11

Segmenting Practise- Rob the Robot Phoneme Frames ................................12

Segmenting Practise- Hide the Words Game ..........................................13

Segmenting Practise- The New Quick Write...........................................14

Spelling Practise- Super Sound Sorter ...............................................15

Segmenting Practise- Change My Spellings ...........................................16

Segmenting Practise- The Elimination Game ..........................................16

Tricky Word Reading Practise- Whole Class Snap! ....................................18

Tricky Word Reading Practise- Stand Up, Sit Down Game .............................19

Tricky Word Spelling Practise- Guess the Missing Letter Game........................20

Applying in a Sentence- Reading ....................................................21

Applying in a Sentence- Writing.....................................................22

Applying in a Sentence- Missing Word Sentences .....................................23

Practise Games for teaching Vowels, Consonants and Syllables .......................24

Vowel Treasure Hunt ...............................................................25

Write the Missing Vowels Game .....................................................26

Consonant / Syllable Counter.......................................................27

Slap the Syllables...................................................................28

Musical Syllables ...................................................................29

Cheerleader Vowel Chant...........................................................30

# Oral Blending & Segmenting Game- What's The Word Mr Wolf?

**What You Need**

This is best played in large space- outdoors is ideal

Objects, picture cards or a list of words containing the focus letter-sound (grapheme-

phoneme)

correspondence)

**What To Do**

Stand at one end of the space as 'Mr Wolf' and explain that all of the children need to stand at the other end of the space (as far away from Mr Wolf as they can, within earshot). This should look like the traditional game of *What's the time Mr Wolf?*

Stand with the cards, objects or words facing away from the children. You may need to enlist the help
of a second adult to join in with the children when they are learning how to play.

The children begin by chanting the phrase "What's your word Mr Wolf?' Mr Wolf calls out one word
from the list / objects /cards selected for the game.

The children need to think about the number of phonemes (sounds) they can hear in the word, then take the corresponding number of steps towards Mr Wolf to segment the word. For example, hand =  h-a-n-d, 4 steps. The children should say each phoneme (sound) as they step.

Play continues in this way, with the children chanting, Mr Wolf calling out a whole word, then the
children saying and stepping out the correct number of phonemes (sounds) in each word.

When the children have almost reached Mr Wolf, and have chanted 'What's your word Mr Wolf?
Mr Wolf shouts out '"Dinnertime"!

The children will then need to run as quickly as they can back to the starting point where they
are safe and ready to play again.

Mr Wolf can 'catch' one of the children. He / she can become the new Mr Wolf as the game begins
again.

Repeat as many times as possible so the children get plenty of practise

# Oral Blending & Segmenting Game – I Hear With My Little Ear

**What You Need**

A collection of objects containing the focus phoneme (real objects are more engaging than picture cards if you can find them)

or photos of real objects on the **Fab Phonics-I Hear With My Little Ear slides** in
The Learning Lady shop

**What To Do**

Make sure the children can see all of the objects Play the game with no more than 3 objects at a time to start with.

Before beginning, remind the children of the name for each object, orally segmenting then blending each item as it is introduced (e.g. sock, s-o-ck). Expect the children to join in with you all together.

Model the game by beginning, "I hear with my little ear, something which sounds like…. s-o-ck".

Remind the children that the clue is for one of the objects in front of them.

Can the children guess the object by orally blending the word back together? Can they segment
the object selected (s-o-ck) too?

Repeat with a number of different objects. If the children are confident, let them have a go at offering the clues.

Remind the children that the clue needs to be for one of the objects they can see.

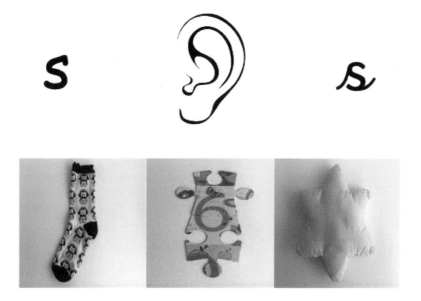

# Oral Blending & Segmenting- Missing Objects 'Magic' Game

**What You Need**

A collection of objects containing the focus phoneme (real objects are more engaging than picture cards) or photos of real objects on the **Fab Phonics Missing Objects Magic Game slides in** The Learning Lady shop

A magic cloth and magic wand

**What To Do**

Make sure the children can see all of the objects. Play the game with no more than 3 objects at a time to start with.

Before beginning, remind the children of what each object is called, orally segmenting then blending each item as it is introduced (e.g. star, s-t-ar). Expect the children to join in with you all together.

Say the names of the objects several times all together to help the children remember the objects in the game; e.g. sock, six, star, sock, six, star...sock, six, star.

Explain that you are going to perform some magic to make one of the objects disappear!

Using the cloth and wand (to cover the real objects if you're using them), say some magic words all together as the children shut their eyes.

If you are using real objects, pick up an object inside the cloth and remove it from the set.

If you are using the slides, move on to the slide with an object missing.

Ask the children to open their eyes then practise saying the remaining items all together as before.  "sock, …….., star"

Can they work out which object is missing? Choose one child to offer an idea.

Can all of the children orally segment the word which is missing all together? (e.g. s-i-x, six).

Repeat several times with all of the children joining in.

Provide a big reveal of the missing object or picture by returning it to the original sequence.

Repeat the game again with further objects, making sure that all children join in, repeatedly saying the names of the objects all together before each one is removed.

# Supermarket Phoneme Spotting Game

**What You Need**

A collection of everyday packaging containing the focus phoneme or a text containing the phoneme or the **Fab Phonics Supermarket Phoneme Spotting slides** in the Learning Lady shop

**What To Do**

Remind the children of the focus grapheme-phoneme (letter-sound) correspondence taught in the session using a flashcard or slide.

Expect the children to join in by reading it all together.

Explain that the children are going to play a game of I Spy- You are going to show them something from your supermarket shopping, and they need to spot the correspondence taught.

Begin the game by chanting, "I spy with my little eye, something which sounds like…. sssssssssss".

Show the children the object, picture or slide chosen for the game. Can the children find the focus letter–sound independently?

Repeat with a number of different items, pictures or pages in a book.

Encourage the children to pay their own game of I Spy through the play provision.

How many examples of today's phoneme can they find in the reading area?

Can they take a photo of the examples they find? Can they continue this game at home?

## Blending Practise- Rob the Robot

### What You Need
Cards with sound buttons matched to the focus phoneme- consistently matched to your whole school approach or **Fab Phonics Rob the Robot Blending Slides** in The Learning Lady shop

You could make your own Rob the Robot (a photocopy paper box is idea). Use standard post it notes to add and subtract the phonemes from Rob's mouth!

### What To Do

Tell the children that they are going to read Rob's words by saying each of the separate phonemes (sounds) as they fly into his mouth, blending them back together to read each whole word

This process is exactly the same if you're using Sound Button Cards- Don't forget to point to the button underneath each separate phoneme. This helps the children to practise saying each phoneme separately before blending them back together to read the whole word.

Expect the children to join in by saying each of the separate phonemes (sounds) as they fly into Rob the Robot's mouth.

Model blending the whole word, with the children joining in all together.

Repeat with further words using either procedure.

# Blending Practise- Speedy Read Game

## What You Need
A list of words including the focus phoneme or tricky words. You could a handwritten list, a set of cards or the **Fab Phonics Speedy Read Slides** in The Learning Lady shop

1-minute timer

## What To Do

Explain that the children are going to play a reading race game. They are going to read all of the words on the list, as many times as they can, in one minute. Explain that all of the children will be joining in all together at the same time.

If you're playing this with a new letter-sound (grapheme-phoneme) correspondence, the children will be expected to read each of **the separate phonemes** (sounds) then blend them back together to read each word. Tricky words will be read as whole words on sight.

Set the timer then attempt to read as many words as possible, all together in one minute, providing a positive model.

Record the score of this first attempt at the end of the first minute. Praise the children for correct articulation of the phonemes and effective blending.

Explain that the children are now going to try to beat their score by reading all of the words on the list again, as many times as they can, in one minute. Explain that on this second attempt the children will be expected to join in all together, reading as quickly as they can.

If you're playing this with a new letter-sound (grapheme-phoneme) correspondence, the children no longer need to say each of the separate phonemes to blend. This is aimed at increasing fluency.

Set the timer then attempt to read as many words as possible, all together in one minute, Hopefully the children will have beaten their original score as fluency increases!

they
my
all
her
they
you
she
all
are
was

# Blending Practise- The Alien Pop Up Game

**What You Need**

A set of word cards containing the focus phoneme. Use a set of relevant cards selected from the Year 1 Phonics Screening materials Or **Fab Phonics Alien Pop Up Game Slides** from The Learning Lady Shop

1-minute timer (optional)

**What To Do**

This is a rapid game and is meant to be active. The children are going to be standing up and sitting down- so make sure they have plenty of space.

Explain that this is a game of real words and alien words (the alien words are words which don't make any sense).

Tell the children that whenever they see a word which is not a real word (an alien word), they need to stand up.

When they read a real word, they need to sit down. The aim of the game is not to be caught out by the aliens!

The game is played by reading through the slides or cards, joining in all together.

Expect the children to read the words as they are shown, saying each of the separate phonemes sounds), then blending them back together to read whole words. Support the children by pointing to each of separate phoneme as they read.

If an alien (non-word) is read, the children need to remember to stand up, otherwise they need to remain seated. Try to catch the children out!

Look, listen and note children who are standing up and sitting down in the right places and maintain a good pace. For extra pace, play against a 1minute timer!

# Blending Practise- Tracking

**What You Need**

Create a piece of text including the focus words you are teaching the children to read and spell. Incorporate the words you're using with strings of letters to 'hide' the words in the jumbled text. Individuals / pairs will need a copy of this text. Or use the tracking texts in The Learning Lady Shop

A list of hidden words to find

Highlighter pens

**What To Do**

This tracking activity works like a wordsearch.

Show the children the words they need to 'track' and point out a key element to help them find the words. For example, present tense verbs ending in *ing* would require the children to look out for i-n-g. words. Words with the ay phoneme would require the children to look out for an *a y*.

Demonstrate how to track from left to right, working along the letters until the first word is found. Highlight the word to show the children how this is done.

Expect the children to work independently, or in pairs, to track down the remaining words using the highlighter pens.

*Wkqopdkwecwjvnevepaintingwj*
*cwwjvnelkiqwhdiuhyrgeaax*
*pointingkekrkekwocwtwiring*
*oejkdsnjveivejvsprayingcnwkjnsa*
*yingkwvjevvjvjnvjeatingwecocen*
*wkmkrtgmrtbrjesnowingsqpqow*
*cwevewvsprayingxqpwpeofruey*

*This is also a great game to play with tricky words and an easy homework takeaway following teaching

# Segmenting Practise- Rob the Robot Phoneme Frames

**What You Need**

1 phoneme frame per child (Rob the Robot is pictured here but it is important to follow the **consistent whole school approach**) This could be a frame including 2, 3 or4 boxes, depending on the phonic phase being taught

Print off a free set of **Fab Phonics Rob the Robot Phoneme Frames** in The Learning Lady shop.

A set of phonemes on post it notes or magnetic letters (as indicated for the words on the weekly plan).

**What To Do**

Tell the children the word they are going to make using the phonemes frames. Orally segment the word a number of times all together, following the chosen whole school procedure (this might include using robot arms or counting on phoneme fingers).

Demonstrate finding the phonemes in the correct order from the selection of post it notes or magnetic letters available, modelling to show that the children always need to start making words from the left.

Place each of the phonemes in a square, one at a time. Expect the children to join in saying the phonemes (sounds) to match the letters as you do so. Read the completed word all together by saying each phoneme separately, then blending them together to read the whole word.

Support the children in making the word independently on their own phoneme frames. Guide the children to correct themselves as appropriate. Can the children say each of the separate phonemes and then blend to read each whole word back? all together?

Repeat the process with further words.

# Segmenting Practise- Hide the Words Game

**What You Need**

Selected words including the focus phoneme / tricky words. You could use printed cards with sound buttons or handwritten words on post it notes or **Fab Phonics Hide the Word Game slides** in The Learning Lady shop

A whiteboard, pen and rubber for each child- this could also be completed in a workbook if preferred.

**What To Do**

Show the children the words for the game, saying each of the separate phonemes (sounds) then blending them back together to read each word. Expect the children to join in all together.

Repeat read all of the words a number of times to help the children remember them.

Explain that you are going to perform some 'magic' by making one of the words disappear.

Remind the children that this is a memory game, so they will need to look very closely and concentrate to remember the words.

Ask the children to close their eyes then say some magic words all together. As the children are doing this, remove a word from the set or move on to the next slide where a word will be missing.

Ask the children to open their eyes to reveal the remaining words. Chant the remaining words all together to work out which is missing. Can the children work out which it is?
Choose somebody to offer an idea.

Orally segment the missing word all together, following the whole school procedure.
This may include strategies such as robot arms or phoneme fingers.

Expect the children to have a go at writing the missing word from memory. Support the children by showing them the phonemes they will need, using a resource which follows the whole school approach. This might include a frieze or letter cards.

Correct letter formation / errors made with appropriately high expectations, particularly looking out for letter reversals.

Deliver a big 'reveal'. This will enable the children to independently check the word written against the original model.

Repeat the process with further words

brown

shout    found

# Segmenting Practise- The New Quick Write

### What You Need

Whiteboard and pens for the practitioner and children. The children could alternatively complete this in workbooks.

1-minute timer

### What To Do

Model writing a word containing the focus phoneme or Tricky Word. If you're teaching words including a new letter-sound (grapheme-phoneme) correspondence, begin by first oral segmenting using the whole school approach (such as counting on phoneme fingers or using robot arms). This is a great opportunity to model the whole school approach to handwriting.

If you're teaching a new Tricky word, make sure you clarify the unusual elements / spelling choices.

Expect the children to join in by reading the word together several times, this will help them to remember. If you're teaching words including a new letter-sound correspondence, model reading each sound (phoneme) separately, then blending them back together to read the whole word.

Explain that the challenge is to write this word as many times as they can in 1 minute, without looking at the model.

Remind the children of the spelling of the word one more time, then hide the word.

Remind the children of where to look if they struggle to remember how to form the letters. This could include referring to a nearby letter frieze or specific letter cards.

Set the timer, expecting the children to independently write the word as many times from memory as they can in 1 minute.

Support with letter formation and accurate segmenting as required.

At the end of minute, show the children the original word. Can they check their writing against the original model?

Repeat with further words (as directed by the weekly plan).

# Spelling Practise- Super Sound Sorter

**What You Need**

A slide / display / frieze which shows all of the spelling rules and alternative pronunciations previously taught (see below)

A grid representing the focus spelling alternatives, or **Super Sound Sorter Slides from** <u>The Learning Lady Shop</u>

A workbook, whiteboard and something to write with

**What To Do**

The children can work independently or in pairs to complete this game.

Teach the children how to organise their board/ page into a grid, with the alternative phoneme choices at the top of each column (see below).

Revisit each of the alternative spelling rules to remind the children of the alternative spelling rules / alternative pronunciations. Say the first word aloud. For example, "rain". Expect the children to join in with segmenting that word orally all together. *R-ai-n.*

*Talk the children through the process of deciding which version of the ai spelling they could choose by thinking aloud as a demonstration. For example:*

*"Is the ai at the end of rain? No, so we don't need ay because that is usually used at the end of words."*
*"Is rain a 2 syllable word? No, so it's unlikely to need an a on its own, that usually happens in words of more than 1 syllable."*
*"Could it be a-e? Possibly because that sounds like it is in the middle of words."*
*"Could it be ai? Most likely because that also happens in the middle of words."*
*"Which looks like the right spelling of rain?" Write down rane and rain?*
Make a choice and write rain in the appropriate column

Provide the children with further words by saying them aloud and expecting them to go through the process demonstrated above. Remind the children of the rules to specifically consider as required.

When the children have sorted and written the words you are using for the game, encourage them to self-correct by showing them the words, sorted by appropriate columns. Talk feedback from individuals and groups. Can the children explain their choices for spellings in relation to the rules they've been taught?

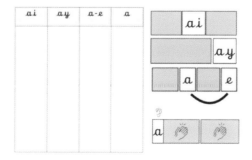

# Segmenting Practise- Change My Spellings

**What You Need**
A slide / display / frieze which shows all of the spelling rules currently being taught (see below)

A slide / worksheet containing misapplication of the spelling rule being taught (see below or visit **The Change My Spellings Slides** in The Learning Lady Shop

1 minute timer

A workbook, whiteboard and something to write with

**What To Do**

Show the children all of the misspelt words, explaining these are not the correct spellings because they don't follow the spelling rule the children have been learning.

Demonstrate with the first word on the list, explaining why the spelling is incorrect, and modelling the correct spelling using the rule prompts that the children have been following. Write the word following the correct rule.

Explain that the children are going to play a timed game against the clock. They have one minute to rewrite all of the words which are misspelt, using the correct spellings which follow the rule.

Set the timer and expect the children to work independently, support / provide feedback as required.

After 1 minute, how many words did the children spell correctly. Provide the correct spellings so that the children can self-correct and evaluate their own spelling choices.

cace
tace
pace
jace
wace
shace
snace
smace
chace
brace
flace

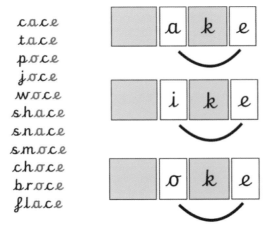

# Segmenting Practise- The Elimination Game

**What You Need**

A slide / display / frieze which shows all of the spelling rules currently being taught (see below)

A 3 x 3 grid of words covering the alternative spelling rules being revised (see below or visit **The Elimination Game Slides** in The Learning Lady Shop

When the children play this game for the first time, it may be helpful for the children to have their own copies of the grid to mark off words as they play. The children could copy the grid onto their own whiteboards and rub words off as the game is played.

**What To Do**

The Elimination Game is like a reverse version of Bingo.

Read through all of the words on the Elimination Game grid all together. Expect the children to join in with reading each of the separate sounds, blending them back together to read the words.

Revisit each of the spelling rules. Can the children find a word on the grid which follows a particular rule? For example:

*"Can you find a word with an ay making the ai sound? Why does this word use ay and not ai?"*
*"Can you find a word which has the a-e split digraph? Can you explain why this a-e is used in this word and not ay?"*

Explain that you are going to choose one of the words on the grid. Write it on a piece of paper / whiteboard but don't show this to the children yet. Explain that you are going to give the children a series of clues for the children to work out what the word is. The children will need to use the clues to eliminate words. For example:

*"The word written on my board does not contain a sh digraph."*
*"The word written on my board does not contain an ay ending."*
*"The word written on my board does not rhyme with pain."*
*"The word written on my board does not contain the two consonants s and c next to each other".*

Make sure the clues represent all areas of teaching previously covered.

Once all clues have been provided. Can the children write down the word which they think is hidden. Provide a big reveal. Does the word that is written down match the words written by the children? If required, go back through the clues using the grid to help the children understand the elimination process.

# Tricky Word Reading Practise- Whole Class Snap!

**What You Need**

Selected tricky words, including the new word introduced. Use printed cards or handwritten words on post it notes or

**Fab Phonics Whole Class Snap slides** in The Learning Lady shop

1minute timer (optional)

**What To Do**

Remind the children of the Tricky Word taught by showing it on the left of a board. If you're using cards, this can simply be handwritten on a whiteboard or displayed on a post it. This remains in place throughout the game.

Explain that this game is like a traditional game of snap. More words will be introduced to the right of the taught word. As the children read these words, they are looking for the same word as the one being introduced (a 'snap' with the word on the left).

Click through the slides or add post it's / cards to the right of the original Tricky Word. As new words are added to the right-hand side of the Tricky Word, the children read the words introduced all together.

When the taught Tricky Word is shown (and matches the word on the left), all of the children shout out "Snap" and win a point.

Play can continue in this way as many times as required. A timer could also be introduced to see how many "snap's' can be identified in 1 minute.

# Tricky Word Reading Practise- Stand Up, Sit Down Game

**What You Need**

A set of Tricky Word cards including the current Tricky Word taught or a set of phonemes cards containing the focus phoneme or

**Free Fab Phonics Tricky Word Stand Up, Sit Down Slides** in The Learning Lady shop

1minute timer

**What To Do**

This is a rapid game and is meant to be active. The children are going to be standing up and sitting down on the spot, so make sure they have plenty of space.

Show the focus word or phoneme card / slide to remind the children of the focus for the game.

Explain that whenever the children see this word / phoneme they need to stand up, for the rest of the game they need to sit down. The aim of the game is not to be caught out.

Begin the game by speedily moving through the slides or cards. Expect the children to join in with reading the words / phonemes as they are shown. They need to remember to stay seated for the words / phonemes which are not the focus of the game.

If the focus phoneme / word is presented the children need to remember to stand up.

Look, listen and note for children standing up and sitting down in the right places and maintain a good pace.

For extra pace, play against a 1minute timer.

# Tricky Word Spelling Practise- Guess the Missing Letter Game

**What You Need**
An enlarged version of the taught Tricky Word, this can be handwritten, on cards or using the **Fab Phonics Guess the Missing Letter** slides in The Learning Lady Shop

This game can also be played using a selected word containing the focus phoneme.

A whiteboard, pen and rubber for each child- this could also be completed in a workbook if appropriate.

1minute Timer

**What To Do**

Demonstrate reading the Tricky Word all together. Take care to clarify the part of the spelling which makes this word tricky.

If you're playing with words including the focus phoneme, model saying each separate phoneme (sound), blending them back together to read the whole word. Now hide the whole word by tuning over the card or moving on to the next slide.

Show the children the same word but with a letter / phoneme missing. Can the children work out which part of the word is missing?

Challenge the children to write the missing letter / phoneme as many times as they can in one minute using the timer. Support with letter formation as required.

Show the children the original word to independently check their writing. Did they remember the correct letter / phoneme? Were the letters / phonemes formed correctly?

Repeat with further missing letters from the same word.

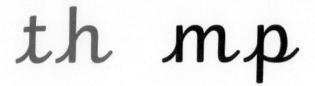

# Applying in a Sentence- Reading

**What You Need**

Whiteboard and pen

**What To Do**

Explain that you are going to write a sentence / caption and you are going to need the children to help with the reading.

Demonstrate writing the first word on the board. Remind the children that you always need to start on the left and, depending on the Phonic Phase, that the sentence needs to begin with a capital letters. Capitals are probably best introduced in Phase 3 when the children are really familiar with some lower-case letters. This will depend on your assessed knowledge of the children.

Read the first word all together, either by blending or reading by sight if it is a Tricky Word. Expect the children to join in.

If it is a word the children are expected to blend, make sure you point to each separate phoneme before blending the whole word back together.

Talk through leaving a finger space before the next word is written. Segment (sound talk) the next word as it is written, expect the children to orally segment all together with you as you write, following the consistent whole school approach (e.g. phoneme fingers / robot arms).

Read back each of the separate sounds, blending all together to read the whole word once it has been written.

Return back to the beginning of the sentence or caption after each word has been added to remind the children.

Reread the words previously written all together before adding the next word to the sentence or caption.

Continue in this manner until the sentence or caption has been fully read all together.

Expect the children to read the whole sentence all together with support, then all together on their own.

Point to each of the words as they are read to demonstrate the direction of reading.

Take the opportunity to model specific letter formation for some letters as you write, following the whole school 'patter' to describe the expected formation.

Only introduce deliberate mistakes when you are confident that the children actually understand what a correct model looks like.

# Applying in a Sentence- Writing

**What You Need**

Whiteboards and pens for each child- this could also be completed in a workbook if appropriate.

Tricky Word / phoneme cards to support memory (these must follow **the consistent whole school approach**)

**What To Do**

Rehearse by saying the sentence / caption the children are going to write aloud, all together.

Repeat several times with the children joining in all together to embed the sentence in the short-term
Memory Include physical actions such as; counting the number of words on their fingers, clapping the sentence with their hands, tapping the words into their brains, stamping the words with their feet.

Explain that the children are going to write the sentence all together at the same time, one word at a time.

Remind the children that writing always needs to start on the left and, depending on the Phonic Phase, that the sentence needs to begin with a capital letter. Capitals are probably best introduced in Phase 3 when the children are really familiar with some lower-case letters, but this will depend on your assessed knowledge of the children.

Remind the children of the first word. Orally segment the word all together at least twice, following the consistent whole school approach (e.g. robot arms or phoneme fingers).

Expect all children to have a go at writing this word, stopping once it has been written by placing a finger space ready to continue.

If the children need to write a tricky word, remind them why the word is tricky and what they need to remember to spell the word correctly. In the early stages it might be appropriate for them to have the support of a Tricky Word card to support.

Revisit the whole sentence by saying it aloud. Reread the word the children have just written. Can they work out what the next word will be?

Continue in this structured manner, segmenting orally, writing, reading new words then re-reading previous words until the sentence or caption is complete.

Expect each child to reread his/her own writing to check that it makes sense.

Support individuals with letter formation and oral segmenting as appropriate.

## Applying in a Sentence- Missing Word Sentences

**What You Need**

A sentence with a missing word displayed, with three alternative words which could fit in the place of the missing word (only one will make sense). Simply write out the sentence with alternative words on posts it notes or use the **Fab Phonics Missing Word Sentence slides** in The Learning Lady shop

Whiteboards and pens or a workbook if appropriate

**What To Do**

Remind the children that all good sentences need to make sense. The sentence shown is not a good sentence because it doesn't make sense, there's a word missing.

Explain that the children are going to read the sentence to work out what the missing word might be. When the right word is added, the sentence will make sense, if the wrong word is added, it won't

Read the first word all together, either by blending or reading by sight if it is a Tricky Word. Expect the children to join in. If it is a word the children are expected to blend, make sure you point to each separate phoneme before blending the word back together.

Follow this process as each word is read. Return back to the beginning of the sentence after each word has been added to remind the children. Reread the words previously read all together until the whole sentence has been read.

Read the three alternatives for the missing word all together. Can the children work out the most suitable word to fill the missing word gap.

Encourage the children to discuss this with a partner then record their choice on a whiteboard.

Demonstrate reading by adding some of the unsuitable words first, with all of the children Joining in as before. Ask the children for their opinions about whether or not the new addition to the sentence makes sense or not.

Finally add the real missing word into the gap in the sentence. Expect the children to read the whole sentence all together, with support, then all together on their own. Point to each of the words as they are read to demonstrate the direction of reading.

Ask the children to check whether or not the sentence finally makes sense, with a thumbs up or thumbs down check.

### Have a go with the ................ said Mum.

| have | paint | burnt |

# Practise Games for teaching Vowels, Consonants and Syllables

## Vowel Spotter

### What You Need
A piece of text, this could include a list of Phase 4 words the children are familiar with, a class list or a piece for text from a decodable book (Phase 4 level) or equivalent.
A workbook or whiteboard & something to write with

### What To Do
Teach the children how to organise their board/ page following this example.

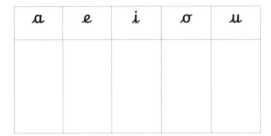

Show the children the text they are going to be using. Show them how to identify the vowels in the first few words. Demonstrate how to write the words to populate the grid.

For example:
The word *crush* would be written in the **u** column because the *u* is the only vowel in that word. The word flapjack would be written in **a** column because there are two *a's* in that word.

Expect the children to work in pairs to read the text, agree on the vowels that they see in the words, writing the words into the appropriate column.

To make this game harder, add in polysyllabic words (words with more than one syllable) which may fit in to multiple columns e.g., laptop.

Try to avoid vowel digraphs (ee, oo, ow, igh etc) until the children are aware that there is more than one way of spelling the same spoken phoneme. For example, using words like *broomstick*, which includes the long vowel **oo**, may be confusing at this point.

# Vowel Treasure Hunt

**What You Need**
As many magnetic letters for single letter phonemes as you can find, or write lots of single letter phonemes on post it notes

Two tubs / buckets / hoops labelled 'vowels' & 'not vowels'

A large space, outside is ideal

**What To Do**
Before the game begins, hide all of the magnetic letters around the space and set up the hoops / buckets / tubs ready for sorting.

Explain that the children are going to go on a treasure hunt to find all of the magnetic letters which are hidden. When a magnetic letter is found the children need to decide if it is a vowel, or if it is not a vowel, then sort it into the correct hoop / bucket / tub.

Set the children off on the treasure hunt, observing as they find and sort the letters found. Add the use of a timer for additional pace and to keep the children on track.

At the end of the game, check through the 'vowels' bucket / hoop / tub all together. Were these letters correctly sorted?

*Adapt this game for teaching consonants too

# Vowel / Consonant Stand Up, Sit Down

**What You Need**
A set of flashcards / slides including only single letter phonemes

**What to do**
Play in the same way as the Tricky Word Stand Up, Sit Down Game on page.

In this vowel version, the children stand up if they see a vowel, and sit down if they see a consonant.

In the consonant version, the children stand up if they see a consonant and sit down if they see a vowel

# Write the Missing Vowels Game

**What You Need**
A list of words from Phase 4 Letters and Sounds, only choose words with short vowels.

There needs to be 2 versions of this list:
A list of the complete words to read
A list of the same words with all of the vowels missing

Whiteboards or workbooks for recording

| | |
|---|---|
| tent | t nt |
| hump | h mp |
| stink | st nk |
| pond | p nd |
| stand | st nd |
| lost | l st |
| strong | str ng |
| spin | sp n |
| bring | br ng |
| crush | cr sh |

**What to do**
Begin by reading all of the words on the complete list all together. Practise saying each of the separate phonemes, then blending them back together to read the whole words.

Explain that all of the vowels are going to disappear from these words, and that the children are going to work together to find out which vowels should go where.

Show the children the words with the missing vowels, hide the complete words. The children work in pairs to work out the missing vowels, discussing their ideas. Explain that they will need to record their ideas by writing the whole words correctly, underlining the vowels that were missing.

At the end of the game, show the children the completed list again. Ask them to look at their own list and correct any words as necessary. Look for examples to provide positive feedback as a model.

# Consonant / Syllable Counter

**What You Need**
A list of words from Phase 4 Letters and Sounds, these can include long vowel digraphs (ee, ow, igh etc) . Use a list of words which becomes progressively more challenging, addressing any previous Phase 3 gaps identified. The children need to be able to see this written list.

A workbook or whiteboard & something to write with

**What To Do**
Teach the children how to organise their board / page following this example.

| 1 | 2 | 3 | 4 | 5 |
|---|---|---|---|---|
|   |   |   |   |   |

Read the list of words all together before beginning, practising saying each of the separate phonemes, then blending them back together to read them.

Explain that the children are going to be consonant counters. They are going to take each word on the list, count up the number of consonants, and then copy the whole word into the column which matches the number of consonants in the word.

For example:
The word *step* has 3 consonants, so *step* would be written in the 3 column.
The word *clear* has 2 consonants, so *clear* would be written in the 2 column.

Demonstrate with a couple of examples before continuing.

Expect the children to work in pairs, discussing their ideas and recording the correct words in the appropriate columns. Support as required.

Go through several completed examples so that the children can begin to self-check their ideas.

*Play this in the same way for counting and sorting the number of syllables in words.

# Slap the Syllables

**What You Need**
A list of Phase 4 and Phase 5 words; some containing 1 syllable, some containing more than 1 syllable. The vowels need to be highlighted in these words. In the early stages, avoid vowel digraphs (e.g igh, oy, a-e) but build up to these slowly over time (see below).

**What To Do**
Remind the children that syllables sound like 'beats' in a word. Demonstrate clapping some syllables in 1 and 2 syllable words as an example.
Cat = 1 syllable
Flip = 1 syllable
Handbag= 2 syllables
Banana = 3 syllables

Explain that the number of 'beats' in words, matches the number of vowels in a word. There is usually one vowel per 'beat'.

**More advanced examples might include:**
Sheep= 1 syllable
daylight= 2 syllables
butterfly= 3 syllables

To play Slap the Syllables, simply show a word (with the highlighted vowel).

Blend to read the word all together

Clap or slap the number of syllables (beats in the word) all together . This can be done on the table, on knees, on the floor, whichever works best.

Repeat using a number of words

# Musical Syllables

**What You Need**

A list of Phase 4 and Phase 5 words; containing 1, and more than 1, syllable. The vowels need to be highlighted in these words. In the early stages, avoid vowel digraphs (e.g igh, oy, a-e) but build up to these slowly over time.

Numbered cards (1,2 and possibly 3, depending on the number of syllables in the words you're using). These need to be attached to cones, walls, fences, spread out in the area you are using.

A large space to play & some music!

**What To Do**

Explain that the children are going to dance to the music and, like in a game of musical statues or 'freeze', when the music stops, the children will need to stand still and listen really carefully.

Play the game up to this point. When the music stops expect the children to 'freeze' and read out the first word. The children should clap the 'beats' or syllables in the word, then run to the number corresponding with the number of syllables counted.

If the children are confident, miss out the clapping stage and expect the children to run to the corresponding number without support.

Show the children the word called, with the vowel / vowels highlighted.
Remind the children that the number of vowels in a word usually corresponds with the number of syllables (see Slap the Syllables for a full explanation). Encourage the children to self-correct. Did they run to the correct number?

Repeat the game in the same way by playing the music, reading a word, children clapping the word, running to the corresponding number, then self-checking by looking at the word all together.

# Cheerleader Vowel Chant

We need the children to know which letters are vowels because many of the Phase 5 spelling rules rely on children knowing what vowels are.

**What You Need**

No resources necessary (although you can jazz this up with some homemade cheerleading pom-poms if you want)!

**What To Do**

Tell the children that they are going to be cheerleaders and that cheerleading involves singing, chanting and actions.

Teach the children the following song, chant and actions by modelling and encouraging them to join in. You will need to practise this several times

Sing to the tune of B-I-N-G-O

The vowels of the alphabet
I know them all by name oh
a-e-i-o-u
a-e-i-o-u
a-e-i-o-u
I know them all by name oh"

Followed by a chant with actions
Teacher: "Give me an a"
Children: "a" (arms above the head in a v shape)
Teacher: "Give me an e"
Children: "e" (arms outstretched)
Teacher: "Give me an I"
Children: "I" (touching toes)
Teacher: "Give me an o"
Children: "o" (two arms stretched out to the left
Teacher: "Give me an u"
Children: 'u" (two arms stretched out to the right)
Teacher: "What have we got?"
Children: "VOWELS" (star jump in the air)

**FREEBIES and much more  – just for you :  )**

**The Learning Lady TES Shop!**

# Teach Phonics SPECTACULARLY well!

## Fab Phonics Online Training is for you if you......

- Are new to Phonics and don't know where to start
- Want to learn about best practice and how you can achieve it
- Have never taught using Letters and Sounds
- Would like a phonics refresher
- Want to up-skill your leadership team or whole school staff
- Are a school governor who wants to learn more

**The most Ideas, advice, top tips and knowledge you'll need to get started straight away!**

**Find out  what you'll learn and what's included.....**

# The Learning Lady

Teaching Alternative Spellings

ee e ea
e-e y ie

Santa's Reading Game

New to Phonics?

Visit The Learning Lady on You Tube!

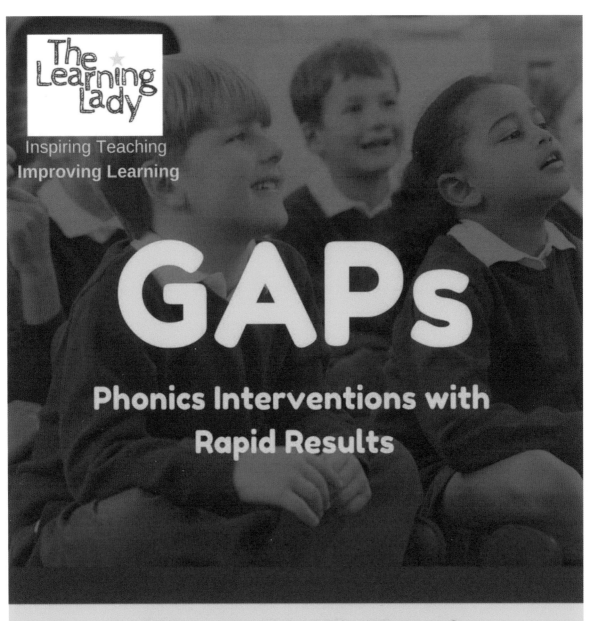

The Learning Lady

Inspiring Teaching
Improving Learning

# GAPs

## Phonics Interventions with Rapid Results

## A KS1 and KS2 Phonics Recovery Programme

## Activities, Planning, Training
## All in one!

Printed in Great Britain
by Amazon